THE WALK

THE WALK

A Journey of A Christian Man

Jason A. Peepas

Library of Congress Control Number:		2019903464
ISBN:	Hardcover	978-1-7960-2340-4
	Softcover	978-1-7960-2339-8
	eBook	978-1-7960-2341-1

Print information available on the last page.

Rev. date: 04/24/2019

To order additional copies of this book, contact:
Xlibris
1-888-795-4274
www.Xlibris.com
Orders@Xlibris.com
794122

CONTENTS

Declaration of Victory 1

Declaration of Victory 2 2

A Declaration of Love 3

Declaration of Who I am.. 4

Declaration of Which I am Part 2 5

Declaration of Who I am Part 3 (in Christ).......................... 6

Declaration of Who I am Part 4 (in Him) 8

Faith Confession 10

Don't Quit..11

Jesus is Walking with you 12

Silence 13

The Call 14

The Cry...15

Thunderous Hooves 16

The Winds of Change...17

The Stand...18

Free...19

We Declare Your Will... 20

Poetry from the Heart 21

Best of Friends... 22

Death 23

For Her... 24

Loneliness 25

Fragmented Heart 26

Tears.. 27

Longing for my soul mate Part 1 (3,000 miles of
heartache)... 28

Longing for my Soul mate Part 2 29

Longing for my Soul Mate Part 3 30

Longing for my Soul Mate Part 4 31

My Heart Urns 32

My feelings for U 33

Twelve Ways To Humble Yourself........................ 34

The Fight 37

The Pain 38

The Gold Nuggets From Heaven............................ 39

The Voice in the wind.. 46

The Path way 48

I have decided 50

Arise 52

Hot off the Press... 53

Hot off the Press... 54

Bearing my Heart.. 55

Hot off the Press... 56

Hot off the Press...57

A song.. 63

Hot off the Press... 64

Forgiveness Prayer 65

Alone again 71

My Meditations... 73

The Winds of Change... 82

The Wind of Change 83

Acknowledgements 91

Scriptures

Joshua 24:15

New King James Version (NKJV)

¹⁵ And if it seems evil to you to serve the LORD, choose for yourselves this day whom you will serve, whether the gods which your fathers served that *were* on the other side of the River, or the gods of the Amorites, in whose land you dwell. But as for me and my house, we will serve the LORD

Ephesians 6:10-17

The Armor of GOD

¹⁰ **Finally, be strong in the Lord and in his mighty power.** ¹¹ **Put on the full armor of God, so that you can take your stand against the devil's schemes.** ¹² **For our struggle is not against flesh and blood, but against the rulers, against the authorities, against the powers of this dark world and against the spiritual forces of evil in the heavenly realms.** ¹³ **Therefore put on the full armor of God, so that when the day of evil comes, you may be able to stand your ground, and after you have done everything, to stand.** ¹⁴ **Stand firm then, with the belt of truth buckled around your waist, with the breastplate of righteousness in place,** ¹⁵ **and with your feet fitted with the readiness that comes from the gospel of peace.** ¹⁶ **In addition to all this, take up the shield of faith, with which you can extinguish all the flaming arrows of the evil one.** ¹⁷ **Take the helmet of salvation and the sword of the Spirit, which is the word of God.**

Declaration of Victory

We declare victory over this land in Jesus name...
For the battle is the Lords
We walk in victory, and power and might in the Lord Jesus
We are washed by the Blood of the Lamb
We are cleansed by the Blood
We are victorious by the Blood of the Lamb
We are the righteous in Christ
We are free from the curses of our forefathers
For we are victorious in Christ Jesus
Amen

DECLARATION OF
VICTORY 2

We declare victory over this land in Jesus Name…
We declare Victory over doubt and unbelief in Jesus Name
We declare Victory in our Finances in Jesus Name

We declare Victory in our Business in Jesus Name
We declare Victory in our Home in Jesus Name

We declare Victory over infirmity in Jesus Name

We declare Victory in our Walk in Jesus Name

We declare Victory over condemnation in Jesus Name

We declare Victory over mistrust in Jesus Name

We declare Victory over foolishness in Jesus Name

We declare Victory by the Blood of the Lamb in Jesus Name

Amen

A Declaration of Love

I declare the Love of God in my heart
I declare the Love of Christ over my life in Jesus name
I declare the love of God in my family's life
I declare the love of God in Christ in my enemy's life
I declare the Love of God to penetrate my brothers and sisters in Christ Jesus
I declare the love of Christ to penetrate the unsaved souls.
I declare the Love of God to penetrate America and its people in Jesus name.
I declare the love of God in Jerusalem and on the tribes of Israel
In Jesus name
Amen

Declaration of
Who I am

I declare I am a new creature
I declare I am a child of God
I declare I am a partaker of His divine nature
I declare I am an imitator of Jesus
I declare I am the light of the world
I declare I am the righteous of God in Christ
I declare I am led by the Spirit of God
I declare I am observing and doing the Lords commandments
I declare I am a son of God
I declare I am saved by grace through faith
I declare I am forgiven
I declare I am justified
I declare I am sanctified
I declare I am redeemed
I declare I am blessed with all spiritual blessings
I declare I am getting all my needs met by Jesus
I declare I am an heir (inheritor) of God and a joint heir
with Jesus
I declare I am above and not beneath
I declare I am kept safe wherever I go
I declare I am redeemed from the hand of the enemy
I declare I am delivered (freed, liberated, released, and saved)
From the powers of darkness

DECLARATION OF
WHICH I AM PART 2

I declare I am doing all things through Christ who strengthens me
I declare I am exercising my authority over my enemy
I declare I am not moved by what I see
I declare I am daily overcoming the devil
I declare I am casting down vain imaginations
I declare I am walking by faith not by sight
I declare I am more than a conqueror
I declare I am bringing every thought captive
I declare I am being transformed by the renewed mind
I declare I am strong in the Lord and the power of His might
I declare I am an over comer by the blood of the Lamb and the word of my testimony
I declare I am establishing God's Word here on earth
I declare I am healed by His (Jesus') stripes
I declare I am a co-laborer together with God
And this is why I am Victorious in Christ
Amen

Psalm 2

> 7.I will declare the decree:
> The Lord has said to Me,
> 'You *are* My Son,
> Today I have begotten You.
> 8. Ask of Me, and I will give *You*
> The nations *for* Your inheritance,

Declaration of Who I am Part 3 (in Christ)

I declare I am justified and made upright and in right standing with God, freely and gratuitously by His grace (His unmerited favor and mercy), through the redemption which is [provided] in Christ Jesus.

I declare [there is] now no condemnation (no adjudging guilty of wrong) for those who are in Christ Jesus, who live [and] walk not after the dictates of the flesh, but after the dictates of the Spirit.

I declare for the law of the Spirit of life [which is] in Christ Jesus [the law of our new being] has freed me from the law of sin and of death.

I declare I am sanctified (made holy) in Christ and I am to be called to be holy

1 Corinthians 1:30
New King James Version (NKJV)
[30] But of Him you are in Christ Jesus, who became for us wisdom from God—and righteousness and sanctification and redemption.
I declare I am in Christ, *I am* a new creation; old things have passed away; behold, all things have become new.

I declare I am a son of God through faith in Jesus Christ.

To know more about IN Christ read…
Romans 3:25, 8:1, 2, 12:5
1 Corinthians 1:2, 30, 15:22
2 Corinthians 1:21, 2:14, 3:14 5:17

2 John 1:9
Amplified Bible (AMP)⁹Anyone who runs on ahead [of God] and does not abide in the doctrine of Christ [who is not content with what He taught] does not have God; but he who continues to live in the doctrine (teaching) of Christ [does have God], he has both the Father and the Son.

DECLARATION OF WHO I AM PART 4 (IN HIM)

I declare John 3:15 & 16 that everyone who believes may have eternal life in him. For God so loved the world that he gave his one and only Son, that whoever believes in him shall not perish but have eternal life.

I declare for in Him I live and move and have my being.

I declare in Him is life an that life is the light of men

I declare He (God) chose me in Him before the creation of the world to be holy and blameless in His sight.

I declare in Him I was also chosen having been predestined according to the plan of Him who works out everything in conformity with the purpose of His will.

I declare I have received Christ Jesus as Lord and I will continue to live in Him.

I declare I am rooted and built up in Him strengthened in faith as I am taught and overflowing with thankfulness.

1 John 2:6

New International Version (NIV)

Whoever claims to live in him must live as Jesus did

1 John 3:6

New International Version (NIV)

No one who lives in him keeps on sinning. No one who continues to sin has either seen him or known him

Him = Jesus

Faith Confession

Faith always has a good report
I walk by faith
And not by sight
I am a faith person
I refuse to doubt
I refuse to fear
I am a faith child of a faith God
My faith works
I always have a good report
I refuse an evil report
I am on God's side
He is on my side
I serve God
I believe God
I believe God that it shall be
Even as it was told to me,
In His Holy Word
God's Word cannot fail
I cannot fail
I am standing on the Word
I am standing on the Promises of God
Hallelujah

Don't Quit

When things go wrong as they sometimes will
When the road you're trudging seems all uphill
When the funds are low and the debts are high
And when you want to smile but you have to sigh
When care is pressing you down a bit
Rest if you must but don't quit
Jesus loves you...

Jesus is Walking
with you

Life is strange with its twists and turns
As every one of us sometimes learn
And many a failure turns about
When he might have won had he stuck it out
Don't give up though the pace seems slow
You may succeed with another blow

Success is failure turned inside out
The silver tint of the cloud of doubt
And you can never tell how close you are
It may near when it seems far
So stick to the fight when you're hardest hit
It's when things seem worst that you
MUST NOT Quit
Stand
Ephesians 6: 10 -13

SILENCE

Silence is deafening
Silence is not silent at all
Silence thunders
Like roaring fighter jets
Or a waterfall
Silence is an oxymoron
Through the thundering of Silence there is
Peace that surpassing mans
Understanding
Through the Silence
There is the tranquility of God
The Father
The Love of the Son
And the Comfort of
The Holy Spirit
Silence is amazing

THE CALL

The pain overwhelming of what I see the responsibility brings me to cry out.
ARRRRRRRRGGGGGGG I cry why me
Why did I get this call, what do YOU see in me,
I do not see, I have seen Heaven and I have seen the bowels of hell. I feel so incompetent so dumb, why so much pain and heart ache? Why did I answer the Call? What is in me? Where is this potential that You see? My heart yearns for me too see what You see in me. Please show me open my eyes to the darkness shine Your Light in my pain. Open this part of Heaven for me. Save me I cry. I cry to be able to see, the greatness with in me.

THE CRY

The Light of God starts to fade
The dark shadows emerge from the depths
Slowly over-taking
The Light dims
The cries of torment arise
The cries out to the Lord quicken
Does He hear?
Does He Listen?
The torment deepens
The pain increases
The scream and plea for Help
Where is the Lord
Begging and pleading for mercy I cry out
Please save me
The pain of the tears hurts my head
The pain of my heart hurts my soul
The thought of loosing my Savior tor my Spirit within
The depths of Hell surrounded me trying to overtake me....
The Cry: Save me Please, Please God....
The tears ran from my heart like a broken dam
The Blood of My Savior started to fall over me
And wash me from my torment
My iniquity, my sin
He heard me
His Love Touched my pain
His love will always Conquer
The torment and pain

THUNDEROUS HOOVES

Can you feel it?
The shaking
The air strong with the smell of horses
The sensation of the strength the power
And magnificence
Four horses riding this way
One White
One Red
One Black
One Pale
The Power of each one radiates around them
The smell is exciting and sickening at the same time
The sight of them brings hope and fear
The Sound of the
Thunderous Hooves
Brings us Home

The Winds of Change

The *Winds of Change* are coming can you feel it
The fear and excitement of the unknown
Can you feel it?
Your body shakes not knowing when
Everyday is it today you think
Your eyes dart to and fro looking seeking
Mind racing faster and faster
The sound of thundering hooves in your head
WHEN
You ask yourself
I know its coming
Anxiety starts rushing in
The feeling gets stronger
A knowing, sensing, longing
When
The knowing you need this
Wind of Change
Come you cry out
Come
Come to me
Where are you??
Swoosh you hear
I AM here My child
Tears role down your cheek
Knowing its time
The Winds of Change
Come to you

THE STAND

5/22/2012

The wounded solider
Kneels before his King
Battered by the battle
Blood splattered on his armor
Dents in the armor
Exhausted but never gives in
Kneels with humility and honor
For he stood because that is all he could do is Stand
[13] Therefore take up the whole armor of God that you may be able to withstand in the evil day, and having done all, to stand. (Ephesians 6:13 New King James Version (NKJV)

FREE

He freed my soul
Through the Blood
Yes, I said the blood
The blood of the Lamb
You have set me free
I am not bound by sin anymore
For I have repented and been baptized
In the name of Jesus
And that has freed my soul
I am no longer a man of the flesh
But a man of God
A fisher of Men
Praise be to God the Father
And His Son Jesus (the Christ)
And the Holy Spirit
AMEN

WE DECLARE YOUR WILL

We declare your will today in our lives
In Jesus name
Your will for us is to prosper
Your will for us is to be Whole
Healed, Delivered
Obedient to Your voice
Your will is Your Word
Your will is Love one another
As Christ Jesus loves us
So we declare Your Will over my life
And the life of my family
In Jesus name.
Amen

This next section is the walk through "hell"

Poetry from the Heart

A Friend:

Someone who care for you
A person you can count on
Someone you can trust

A friend will always tell you like it is
Never put you down and will always be around

A friend is someone like you
Who I care for very much
You didn't judge me
You accepted me for who I am
And not what I look like

We met only a while ago
But can trust you with my life
You taught me who I am and
To follow Jesus with my heart
You're the best friend I could have

You've been an inspiration
And someone I can really talk to

Once in a great while do friends like you come around.
You're so generous and loving
Where would I be without you?
Thank you for being my friend.

Best of Friends

A day ago we play in the fields
Going thru life as best of friends
Thinking that we know all about the other person
But do we truly know them?

Now that we are older, are we still thinking of each other?
Even though none has called each other

Then one afternoon you get a call
It is from the hospital saying your friends'
Been hurt in a car accident

Then you think of all the good times
and some of the bad ones too,
Still thinking why I didn't call,
Now he might die
Best of friends

DEATH

What is death?
Is it the darkness around us?
When we sleep
Or
Is death a person waiting to
Grab us when we are not paying attention
Or
Is death a spirit?
Know one really knows Death
Till "it" comes for you

FOR HER

For her _____
Love is soft pastel
Layer upon layer
Shifting, mutating, smudging

For Her____
Tears are cold, yet gentle
Reeking with change
Erasing
Cleaning
The vibrant painting
Is Beautiful
Though still missing you

LONELINESS

Is the pain in your heart.
When
There is a bunch of people around
And no one notices you
Loneliness is when your
Married and you live in two different worlds
And you feel that there is no attraction toward you
Loneliness is the most painful of all
Pains
It leads to death.

FRAGMENTED HEART

Heart you are fragmented
Split in many pieces
A piece here a piece there
Where do I find the wholeness?
Is there a fire strong enough to melt me?
Back into one heart not fragmented.
Does that mean the love is fragmented also?
Please send me that special someone that can melt me
Put together the fragmented heart.

TEARS

The tears in my eyes have longed for you.
But when you said no my heart drops and the
tears started rolling, for we got along so well.
For when I found you, you were hurt and I made you happy.
I gave my heart out and all you did was make the tears.

LONGING FOR MY SOUL MATE PART 1 (3,000 MILES OF HEARTACHE)

The pain of heartache sets in
It's like a flat of concrete over my heart
Where there was joy it is now sorrow and despair

For the heart aches for its companion
The soul cries out for his mate,
But no reply
3,000 miles of Heartache

The knots in the stomach tightens as the
Dawn arouse
Sorrow hit and hit hard for
He longs for his soul mate to return

LONGING FOR MY SOUL MATE PART 2

3,000 miles of heartache are now gone
For I was looking in the wrong places
For my soul mate died for me
So I might live
For my soul mate called for me,
But I had no ears to hear

But one day my ears got opened
And heard my soul mate call me
And drew me in,
And broke the slab of concrete off my heart
With the Power of Love
Then and only then could I see my wife.

Longing for my Soul Mate Part 3

As I long for my soul mate
(Only 10-20 feet away)
In the next room fighting to find Love

The Love she seeks is eternally with her,
In our Lord Jesus Christ

The love I have for her is but only a moment
For I am only a sojourner in this world
My time is short
Maybe a minute or an hour for only God knows
For His days are like a thousand years to our one
It is time we take this eternal love with in
And show it toward one another
For we never know the time He may call us home.
For we are sojourners here just passing through
The Longing of my soul mate to sojourn with me,
I still long

LONGING FOR MY SOUL MATE PART 4

I long for
Love that is real from a human
Were is that love
The love of the soul mate
Is it a real thing?

MY HEART URNS

My heart urns for my wife
As I cry out she does not hear
My heart breaks as I cry out to Jesus
I ask were is she Lord
And no response
She is estranged from my spirit
I cry for unity and for her to be beside me but I fight alone
Were is the one You gave to me the one that is supposed
to be with me and Know me by the Spirit of God
My heart breaks for her too know me and for
her to realize I need her in the Spirit
We are supposed to be one not two
Why is it so hard for you to be with me
Am I that bad of a husband and leader she does
not want to fight for me as I did her??
Please God answer me

My heart and soul cry out to You for answers.......

My feelings for U

My feelings for U are so strong
I've had these feelings for so very long
No one knows how I feel inside
My feelings get only stronger because U are my pride

My feelings can be stronger than a hurricane
The thing I love most is when you say my name
My feelings are as strong as they can be
And this my love I will prove to thee

I show my love when we make love
It's like a sign from the heavens above
It makes are bodies tingle with pleasure
It's a feeling U wish would last forever

My feelings for U will never die
And to prove my love I will never lie
And if one day I break thy promise to thee
I'll prove my love again, U'll see

Now I know our love will last, future, present, even past
I'll take things slow, and never fat
My feelings for U will always be true
To say these three words "*I Love U*"

Twelve Ways To Humble Yourself

Routinely confess your sin to God. (Luke 18: 9-14). All of us sin and fall short of the glory of God. However, too few of us have a routine practice of rigorous self-honest examination. Weekly, even daily review of our heart and behavior coupled with confession to God, is an essential practice of humility.

Acknowledge your sin to others. (James 3:2, James 5:16). Humility before God is not complete unless there is humility before men. A true test of our willingness to humble ourselves is being willing to share with others the weaknesses we confess to God. Wisdom, however, dictates that we do so with others that we trust.

Take wrong patiently. (1 Peter 3:8-17). This has been a difficult one for me. When something is unjust I want to react and rectify it. However, patiently responding to the unjust accusations and actions of others demonstrates our strength of godly character and provides an opportunity to put on humility.

Actively submit to authority—the good and the bad! (1Peter 2:18). Our culture does not value submission, rather it promotes individualism. How purposely and actively do you work on submission to those whom God has placed as authorities in your life? Doing so is a good way to humble yourself.

Receive correction and feedback from others graciously.
(Proverbs 10:17, 12:1). In the Phoenix area, a local East valley pastor was noted for graciously receiving any negative feedback or correction offered. He would simply say, "thank you for caring enough to share that with me, I will pray about it and get back to you." Look for the kernel of truth in what people offer you, even if it comes from a dubious source. Always pray, "Lord, what are you trying to show me through this?"

Accept a lowly place. (Proverbs 25: 6-7). If you find yourself wanting to sit at the head table, wanting others to recognize your contribution or become offended when others are honored or chosen, then pride is present. Purpose to support others being recognized, rather than you. Accept and look for the lowly place, it is the place of humility.

Purposely associate with people of lower state than you are, (Luke 7:36-39). Jesus was derided by the Pharisees for socializing with the poor and those of lowly state. Our culture is very status conscious and people naturally want to socialize upward. Resist the temptation of being partial to those with status or wealth.

Choose to serve others. (Philippians 1:1, 2 Corinthians 4:5, Matthew 23:11) When we serve others, we are serving God's purpose in their lives. Doing so reduces our focus on ourselves and builds the Kingdom of God instead of the Kingdom of self. When serving another cost us nothing, we should question whether or not it is really servant hood.

Be quick to forgive. (Matthew 18: 21-35). Forgiveness is possibly one of the greatest acts of humility we can do. To forgive is to acknowledge of a wrong that has been done us and also to further release our right of repayment for the wrong. Forgiveness is denial of self. Forgiveness is not insisting on our way and our justice.

Cultivate a grateful heart. (1 Thessalonians 5:18) The more we develop an attitude of gratitude for the gift of salvation and life He has given us, the truer our perspective of self. A grateful heart is a humble heart.

Purpose to speak well of others. (Ephesians 4: 31-32). Saying negative things about others puts them "one down' and us "one up". a form of pride. Speaking well of others edifies them and builds them up instead of us. Make sure, however, that what you say is not intended as flattery.

Treat pride as a condition that always necessitates embracing the cross. (Luke 9:23). It is our nature to be proud and it is God's nature in us that brings humility. Committing to a lifestyle of daily dying to self and living through Him is the foundation for true humility.

THE FIGHT

The turmoil within I can feel,
The fight for life is real.
I can feel it on the inside of my being
The darkness surrounds me taunting
me, sin gets ever closer.
Thoughts of finding one who will
show me love and affection,
Fighting to find the love I deserve, in a spouse but
only find lack, so the darkness moves ever closer.
I wonder is it because when I look inside, all I see is
this hideous creature with barbs growing thicker?
So the fight inside intensifies
Crying out were the affection a man needs from a spouse?
The answer I get go to Jesus
So I feel that hideous creature rise
from the depths of darkness,
And lashes out from the pain from
the Lack of human touch.
The fight within grows ever stronger
Questions arise am I to be tortured all my days as a human?
Hells flames seem ever closer and closer for the lack
of touch brings sin ever closer and more tempting
One last cry to God, my last call
Can I please have a spouse who will
show me love and affection?
The fight in me is almost gone....
The Black flames have almost consumed me
DEATH is coming.......

THE PAIN

7/20/13
7:53pm

The Pain inside my heart is overwhelming
I ask myself is this fight worth it?
I am sick of fighting
The anger, rage of seeing so much Hypocrisy
in the so called House of God
As tears role down my face I look up and ask
Is this life really worth all this pain?
No love, no affection just the pain of so much
backstabbing in the House of God
I can not handle this pain I cry out
But am I heard? (I don't think so anymore)
I wonder if anyone truly cares.
I hear people's words but their action is just the opposite.
I ask myself would anyone miss me.
The only thing that came to mind was
maybe the inmates might
But oh well
Is this Pain of the fight really worth it?

THE GOLD NUGGETS FROM HEAVEN

This section of the book is a computation of words and visions from God, they are not in order per say. But do hope this does inspire you to search and seek out God, and ask Him to speak to you like this and open your heart up to be able to hear His voice.

April 16,2003
8:15 am

Jason, I made you for this time. I gave you a strong woman so you can learn to trust women. Her heart is pure and righteous. I gave her the same vision. So trust her as you trust ME.

Jason I made you so you can help people understand the process.
The pain is longsuffering and will build your character, and to trust in Me for your healing. Trust your wife I have given you. Let her lead you till you get strong enough to lead her the way.

I have made you to lead her and other people.

Your Loving
Father

While I was waiting upon the Lord to speak to me, I heard the bathroom sink running.

I heard the Lord say: Drink
Don't stop drinking of Me for I Am the Living Water. Your time is almost here (don't give up) to be launched into your ministry.
Keep the faith and the promises I have told you. I AM a God that does not lie.

May 29, 2004
0700

Let the Son shine in your cloudy day.
Let the Son shine thru and break the haze.
Let it burn it away.
Feel the warmth of My Love. Embrace Me this day.
Take My yoke for it is Light.

5-1-05
7:58 pm

My children I long to fellowship with you.
Surrender yourselves to Me.
Come to Me with your burdens,
And take My yoke for it is Light
Take My yoke and be free this night.

6-9-05
10:30 am
(Jason's Dream)

Jason Saw a (lily) purple flower in a meadow setting
A brook of running water
Then waterfalls (Rain forest)
And then Jason was under water (clear
water with beautiful stones/rock)
(Scene changes)

Deep in forest a bearded man getting baptized in water,
Then was walking (with someone) by
the water and the two bowed
But would not look up (out of water)
Jason continued to walk on and saw a bearded
man lying down with arms out stretched
From this point Jason began to ascend in
the clouds like going thru a tunnel

June 23
11 am

Vision in Prayer
Blue sky and then
A cup upright falling
From the sky
Then turned on side (like it was pouring out)
After that came a graduation cap
Done

Tell My people I Am
Assembling My army
Here in heaven
To come join My army on earth
Tell them what you see

I (Jason) saw a banner (streamer)
Like that of old,
And on the hill I saw
A white horse and a man (Jesus)
Looking at His army
Legion upon legions

12-28-06
12:53 pm

Be patient My children wait just a little
Longer and I will endue you with power,
That you have been crying out for;
Embrace MY fire and be consumed
Be consumed from the inside out
With Holy Fire,
Purifying
Cleansing
With Righteousness
Sayth the Lord
No more days
Minutes and hours
I will return for My people the
Remnant
The Sword has been drawn
And I ride
So be vigilant for the time draws nigh
Sayth the Lord

It was about 9:30 and I went and laid
down and I saw blackness.
Debra (my wife) read some scriptures and then
I saw a light and it lit up the darkness.
And I was in a pit coming out.
Then I felt a physical tug on my leg and I was jerked
back. Then I saw myself hanging onto a ledge with the
pit under me, a chain is in the middle of the pit, with a
demon smirking at me and started cutting the chain with
its talons. Then I saw myself jump up and grab onto the
part that was not cut and the demon tried to grab my
leg and I moved out of the way, and began climbing.
That is all I saw done. 12-28-06

As I was looking toward the ocean the break of day started.
God once touches me with love and beauty of simplicity of
a "Sonrise".
I sit and look out my window and I watch the darkness fade
away.
I sense in my spirit that is what He is doing in me.
Making His Son rise up with in me, so people can see His Son
thru me.
Light abounds in the front of me and darkness behind.
Why do I look behind where I can not see?
For in darkness there is no Light. You are blind and can not
see or you see amiss.
It's kind of like the scripture that says something about you
ask but you ask amiss.
As I look around Light now abounds. How great is our God?
That He uses His own creation to talk to His son.
Now if I could just walk that way all the time. I may believe I
was His son.
For my actions have not lined up with His word which is Gods'
only begotten Son,
Jesus the Christ, my Savior and King

THE VOICE IN THE WIND

9-6-05
8:45-9:15 am

The trumpet has been blown by My
Watchmen
Sayth the Lord
The warning of the Lord has come upon you
more than once.
When will you Obey My Voice?
Sayth the Lord
Repent you stiff neck generation
Of all your immorality,
And Religion
Let My Spirit flow and see
My Mighty Hand work
My children time is short
Heed My warning from My
Prophets
Sayth the Lord
Open your hearts unto Me
For I am coming soon

Weekend of June 4th and 5th 2005

I would like to enlighten you about the weekend of
June 4th and 5th 2005. I learned a valuable lesson that
weekend about (rest) being still and knowing that
I AM is GOD. Scripture psalm 46:10.
And about letting go of things in my life.

———

It was refreshing less taxing in the spirit.
This gave God the chance to work in
me and my household. (amen)
Now think what you need to let go of?
The Lord spoke to me and said....
I feel your pain; please do not carry any hurt any
longer. Through My pain on the cross for your sins, I
paid for all your hurts and wounds forever. Therefore,
bring to Me your pain and sorrows I will take them
unto My cross. Even as the eternal clock is ticking
My cross is still available today even through My
Physical suffering on this earth *till it's* over.
My eternal provision for your healing is forever and ever.
Come unto Me and receive your rightful
inheritance divine healing. I feel your pain.

1 peter 2:24

7/27/2012
4:00 am

Kings and Priests do you not hear the call?
The trumpets are being blown.
The enemy's attacks are getting more precise against us.
Rise up do not sit down for Heaven
has taken enough violence.
Now get violent in the Spirit and rise up
and fight which means Pray.
Open your mouths and declare.
For I know the thought I have for you says the
Lord, thoughts of peace and not evil
to give you a future and a hope.

THE PATH WAY

House Scriptures Part 2
Call to Apostleship (Gal 1)

[11] But I make known to you, brethren, that the gospel which was preached by me is not according to man. [12] For I neither received it from man, nor was I taught *it,* but *it came* through the revelation of Jesus Christ.

Isaiah 41

[8] "But you, Israel *(Jason,) are* My servant,
Jacob whom I have chosen,
The descendants of Abraham My friend.
[9] *You* whom I have taken from the ends of the earth,
And called from its farthest regions,
And said to you,
'You *are* My servant,
I have chosen you and have not cast you away:
[10] **Fear not**, for I *am* with you;
Be not dismayed, for I *am* your God.
I will strengthen you,
Yes, I will help you,
I will uphold you with My righteous right hand.'
[11] "Behold, all those who were incensed against you
Shall be ashamed and disgraced;
They shall be as nothing,
And those who strive with you shall perish.

¹² You shall seek them and not find them—
Those who contended with you.
Those who war against you
Shall be as nothing,
As a nonexistent thing.

¹³ For I, the LORD your God, will hold your right hand,
Saying to you, 'Fear not, I will help you.'

1/03-07 *Home Scriptures Part 3*
ARISE

Joshua 1
New King James Version (NKJV)

God's Commission to Joshua

² "Moses My servant is dead. Now therefore, ***arise***, go over this Jordan, you and all this people, to the land which I am giving to them—the children of Israel. ³ Every place that the sole of your foot will tread upon I have given you, as I said to Moses

⁵ No man shall *be able to* stand before you all the days of your life; as I was with Moses, *so* I will be with you. I will not leave you nor forsake you. ⁹ Have I not commanded you? Be strong and of good courage; do not be afraid, nor be dismayed, for the LORD your God *is* with you wherever you go."

I HAVE DECIDED

To stand up for Jesus my King
To stand on the Word of God
To stand up for righteousness
To do the works of my Father in Heaven
To heal the sick & broken hearted
To cast out demons in Jesus name
To raise the dead
I have decided to walk in my God given authority as His son
I have decided to be the King& Priest
that Jesus has called me to be
I have decided not to let the devil win
I have decided that my soul belongs
to God and His kingdom
I have decided to demonstrate the love of Christ to my
brothers and sisters in Christ and to the unbelievers
I have decided to be an imitator of Christ Jesus
I HAVE DECIDED
Have YOU

5/14/2014

Hot off the Press
As I sit and worship You
Your Love overwhelms me as You overtake me
I can't help as tears roll down my face
Knowing the sacrifice you have made for me
The thorns in Your head
The ripped open flesh off Your back
The Blood soaked ground
Just so I can be Redeemed back to the Father
To be able to go back home where I came from
Your sacrifice of Love still overwhelms me

Jeremiah 1:5

Before I formed you in the womb I knew[a] you,
before you were born I set you apart;
I appointed you as a prophet to the nations."

John 3:16
[16] For God so loved the world that he gave his
one and only Son, that whoever believes in
him shall not perish but have eternal life.

———
51

ARISE

5/16/2014

Arise oh Lord, Arise o Lord
Come to our defense o Lord
Come to our defense
Arise o Lord Arise o Lord
Light our Fire Lord, Light our Fire

Arise in us o Lord Arise in us

Let us be Your Kings & Priests o Lord
Let us be Your Kings & Priests

Arise o Lord Hear our cry o Lord
Make Haste to me my King
Make haste to me…

A song from the heart

HOT OFF THE PRESS

5:12pm
6/14/14

Cry out to My Children Cry out
For My ear is turned to you
I AM her to free you from those burdens;
those burdens are not for you to carry
Come to Me let me free you of those chains of false burdens

Cry out to Me for I Am here in this place

The time is NOW
Says the Lord

7:20am
7/8/2014
Hot off the Press

My Love
My Love is Everlasting
Today Receive My Love
My Love is what hold everything together
My Love is My SON
Open your hearts to Him and let Him in
My Love is the Light in the Darkness
My Love is the Light of the universe
Receive My Love

Sincerely
ABBA Father

Hot off the Press

5:17am
7/10/2014

Dear Children,
Harken unto Me time is short
Come to Me while I may be found. Do not let
this world over take you, for it is all passing
away, Gird yourself in the most Holy Faith
Turn you ear to Me Sayth the Lord

Let My Holy Spirit comfort and guide you
Know this My children, put your trust in Me
Put no confidence in flesh
For My Love is eternal, Choose Love
and your Life will be Abundant

Loving
Father

Bearing my Heart

The Lord is my Light and salvation
The Lord is my Buckler and shield my fortress which I run
The Lord is my refuge and strength
The Lord is my Love and Husband
The Lord is my King and friend
The Lord is my Healer
The Lord is my Strength
The Lord is my Heart
The lord is the lamp unto my feet
The Lord is the Light unto my Path
The Lord is my Life which is continually in Your hands
The Lord is teaching me His judgments
The Lord is teaching me His ways
The Lord is purging me with Hyssop
The Lord is washing me so I shall be whiter than snow
The Lord is creating a clean heart
The Lord is renewing a steadfast Spirit within me
The Lord is restoring the Joy of Salvation and
is upholding me by His Generous Spirit
The Lord is given me a broken spirit and contrite heart
The Lord is delivering me from the strivings of people
The Lord is making me the Head of nations
The Lord is Blessing me with
Great deliverance He gives to His king,
And shows mercy to His anointed,
To David and his descendants forevermore.
Amen

HOT OFF THE PRESS

1:36pm
7/26/14

This I say;
Come back to Me My children
Come back to your first Love
Remember this: *Before I formed you in the womb I knew you.*
You are My Beloved come harken unto the leading of My
Spirit,

Says the Lord

I love you My children I long for your fellowship,
Seek Me while I may be found

AMEN

Revelation 2 New King James Version (NKJV)

Hot off the Press

10:25
7/27/14

The Wind of My presence is here
Today is your day to fly/soar Higher in Me
Deliverance is here this day Receive, Receive your freedom
Freedom to soar.
The bondage & chains are broken
Soar My children Soar higher, higher, higher in Me
Says the Lord.

5:15pm
8/03/2014

While in prayer with a sister in the Lord I see:
A stampede of horses a white one leading them, then
the white horse shakes his head and the other horses
split up half on the right and the other half to the left.
Then the white horse came where he was all I could
see. As I looked upon this horse it looked like an
Angel behind him. I was told to get on and the horse
had wings and I was flying on this horse (Pegasus)
When I got on the horse with wings the sky changed
into night, I was seeing white puffy clouds.
I now see a black horde in war armor with a dark
rider on it wings a black as night, and had a legion
behind him all black hordes of demonic soldiers.
As I flew over them it looked like the hordes of hell.
The horde walking had long spears, the ones on
horses had swords. There is small groups scattered
in between the bigger soldiers with small bows.
I the Lord of Hosts show this to you to warn My army
to ARISE to fight in the Spirit, Pray in My Holy Spirit
with power & might. If you stay quiet the enemy will
overtake you. If you open your mouth and Declare
% Decree My Word I will fight for My children.
For I AM the Lord of Hosts.

10/30/2014

~A Word in season for My beloved~
I hear the wind of change,
The wind of fire is here to
consume you......
Let Me engulf you
with the fire of My
Ru-ach Ha-Ko-desh
(Holy Spirit)
Hunger and thirst after My Presence
says Adonai......
I will answer you-
I Adonai Elohim Love you,
with an everlasting Love.
Receive My fullness I have for you.
Come to Zion My holy Habitation
says Adonai.........

7/8/14
7:20am

My Love

My Love is Everlasting
Today Receive My Love
My Love is what holds everything together
My Love is My Son
Open your hearts to Him and let Him in
My Love is the Light in the Darkness
My Love is the Light of the Universe
Receive My Love

Sincerely
Abba Father

6:15am
8/10/2014

I long to be free of this torment and pain, Free to fly free and soar with My King. The shackles of this bondage I need to be free of, Jesus my King come rescue me please, Free me from my tormentors. My heart yurns to get these chains off...
Break every chain, Avenge me My King, Hear my cry oh Lord I am overwhelmed, I cry day and night to you. Hear me I plead with you my Lord and Savior I need Freedom

6:45
8/10/14

Today my I have seen my enemy…. A principality I call you out Jezebel, I am no Ahab. I am of the Lineage of King David of the Tribe of Judah, I am of the Joshua generation, the double portion anointing of Elisha generation. I declare and Decree according to Gods Word your chains over my life are broken by the Death of my King, Lord and Savior Jesus Christ and His Blood that was shed for me set me free from your hold. I will not go back into bondage, I plea the Blood of Jesus of myself and against you. I break every hold off my life that you ever had on me in Jesus name. The Chains are broken the chains are broken…. I am free, I am free because of my KING. I am a mighty Warrior for my GOD Jehovah and no weapon formed against me will prosper.
Vengeance is mine says the Lord.
I will prosper and not die, for the Lord has arose the Warrior within and endued me with the FIRE of the Holy Spirit, As a Son of God, a co air with Christ I call the Holy Fire down on you, you foul spirit You are bound and cast out and never to come back in Yeshua's Name.

A SONG

A do nai, oh A do nai my Lord & King
Can you hear your servant calling
Is your ear inclined to my voice oh A do nai
My heart Yearns for Your presence
A do nai, A do nai A do nai my Lord
A do nai, A do nai A do nai my King
A do nai, A do nai A do nai

HOT OFF THE PRESS

6:01
7/22/2014

What type of vessel are you or what type of vessel do you want to be?

In 2 Timothy it talks about 6 different kinds of vessels (Gold & Silver), (wood, earth) (Honor and Dishonor)

Now this all goes back to whom you will serve God or self (mammon).

Aright, listen to this if your hearts true desire is to serve God you will do this part in 2 Timothy 2:21

[21] If a man therefore purge himself from these, he shall be a vessel unto honor, sanctified, and meet for the master's use, *(which is Christ)* and prepared unto every good work.

As you see it is a choice to be a Gold or Silver vessel (honor). We as believers do not have to stay as wood & earth vessels (dishonor)

Choose to Purge yourself with Holy Fire to be all that God the Father (Abba) wants you to be.

Prayer: Lord Jesus give me the hearts, desire to be a vessel of Gold & Silver (Honor).

The strength and courage to let Your Holy Spirit Fire purge me to be that vessel of honor You want me to be

In Jesus Name Amen

FORGIVENESS PRAYER

Dear Heavenly Father, it is my choice today to forgive (write in name)_____ for the
following offense which he/she brought against me _____(describe offense briefly).
I forgive him/her unconditionally for the things done which brought hurt in my life. I drop every charge
I have brought against him/her and give up right to ever charge him/her again for this offense.
I cancel every judgment I have made against him/her. In the name of my Messiah Yeshua I release
him/her from all responsibility for the hurt which she/he caused me regardless of how badly I was hurt.
Heavenly Father I drop every charge I've had against You for permitting this to happen to me and please forgive me for any way I have blamed you in this offense.
Heavenly Father, as I have forgiven _____ for the hurt I experienced, please forgive me of my hurt, bitterness, anger and unforgiveness (judgments, vows etc.)
Holy Spirit please come and heal my thoughts, my emotions, and my memories from all the damage
and defilement caused by my offense. Thank you, Father, for my healing.
In Yeshua's name, Amen.

It may be necessary to pray more than once, just continue, til you have peace............

Breaking Soul Ties
Yeshua,

I have been looking to another human being to fix the need and the pain inside of me.
I have not made right choices and kept my relationship with this person in proper perspective.
I want to be free from any emotional, intellectual, or self-willed ties I've let form, and I repent
for allowing this to happen. Forgive me for having sought satisfaction and fulfillment from anyone
other than you.

I now loose, cut, and sever any and all soul-ties I have willingly or ignorantly entered into. I reject
these soul-ties and every soulish satisfaction they have provided for me. I loose them, reject them,
renouncing them and every wrong agreement I have ever come into that birthed those soul-ties in
the first place.
I bind myself to the truth of your love, care, faithfulness, mercy, and grace. Your grace is sufficient
for all my needs, hurts, and issues. I am choosing to bring my needs and vulnerabilities to you alone.
I will no longer let fear overcome me when I feel defenseless and vulnerable.
Instead I will remember that this means I am in a place where my souls walls and defense systems
are down. I choose now to realign my thinking and confess out of my mouth, this is not a bad place
to be, Yeshua, I receive your healing and peace.
It is a good place to meet you- here on top of the fallen defenses and tumbled down walls.
I will quickly call out to you to come as deep into my soul as you can, touching every dark spot

with your grace and mercy.

This trust and vulnerability can be used as an open door to your grace, God no matter how quickly

my soul may try to reestablish protective bars over it, I will not hesitate to run to the open door towards

you.

For I'm not sure what finally tore down the defenses I've been building, there will be a time when they

are completely gone, when my soul completely surrenders to you and as long as I stay in your perfect will, they will never return.

I want to be free to love you and others daily, unconditionally.

Yeshua, I've tried too long and too unsuccessfully to get my own soulish, human expectations

fulfilled. Increase my awareness of old patterns of behavior I need to loose. Increase my awareness

of the wrong thinking I need to loose and reject. Increase my awareness that I can trust you with

everything I let you get close to. Help me to recognize every high thing I've allowed my soul to put

up between me and you, and I WILL PULL THEM ALL DOWN!!!!!!

Read Jeremiah 31:1-5

BURACH HASHEIM ADONAI!

SHOW ME YOUR GLORY................I will bring praise and thanksgiving and shout of Your

marvelous works!!!

REBUILD this temple for Your honor and YOUR GLORY!!!

I pray this all in YESHUA'S Name

AHHHHHH MENNNNN!!!!

5:15pm
8/03/2014

While in prayer I see:

A stampede of horses a white one leading them, then the white horse shakes his head and the other horses split up half on the right and the other half to the left.

Then the white horse came where he was all I could see. As I looked upon this horse it looked like an Angel behind him. I was told to get on and the horse had wings and I was flying on this horse (Pegasus)

When I got on the horse with wings the sky changed into night, I was seeing white puffy clouds.

I now see a black horde in war armor with a dark rider on it wings a black as night, and had a legion behind him all black hordes of demonic soldiers.

As I flew over them it looked like the hordes of hell. The horde walking had long spears, the ones on horses had swords. There is small groups scattered in between the bigger soldiers with small bows.

I the Lord of Hosts show this to you to warn My army to ARISE to fight in the Spirit, Pray in My Holy Spirit with power

& might. If you stay quiet the enemy will overtake you. If you open your mouth and Declare & Decree My Word I will fight for My children.

For I AM the Lord of Hosts.

6:45
8/10/14

Today my I have seen my enemy…. A principality I call you out Jezebel, I am no Ahab. I am of the Lineage of King David of the Tribe of Judah, I am of the Joshua generation, the double portion anointing of Elisha generation. I declare and Decree according to Gods Word your chains over my life are broken by the Death of my King, Lord and Savior Jesus Christ and His Blood that was shed for me set me free from your hold. I will not go back into bondage, I plea the Blood of Jesus of myself and against you. I break every hold off my life that you ever had on me in Jesus name. The Chains are broken the chains are broken…. I am free, I am free because of my KING. I am a mighty Warrior for my GOD Jehovah and no weapon formed against me will prosper.

Vengeance is mine says the Lord.

I will prosper and not die, for the Lord has arose the Warrior within and endued me with the FIRE of the Holy Spirit, As a Son of God, a co air with Christ I call the Holy Fire down on you, you foul spirit You are bound and cast out and never to come back in Yeshua's Name.

ALONE AGAIN

As I awoke this morning asking God for the scripture for the day, all I feel is rejected, unwanted and most of all unloved, still no affection from the one who is supposed to be my wife. I do all that I have for her but still not enough, alone in the Spirit and the natural I am. I know my king &Lord are still there/ here. Alone I feel for nothing is good enough for her; so once again I fight temptation, knowing what scripture says: I fight for my life with no help unless I bow down to her will. Which I will NEVER Again bow to Jezebel the controller. So Alone again with my King crying with a scattered shattered heart asking why…Why am I with someone who pretends to care, Why did you tell me to go back when I am so unhappy. Why Father/Abba why do you allow her to hurt me so much WHY?

11/14/15
A New Break thru in Prayer

The "ROAR" of the Lion comes forth with Power & Authority in the Heavens. God's Spirit is conformation.

The movement in the Spirit was war like, the move was like swaying trees in the wind.

The peace of God is overwhelmingly thick, first time in a long time the Reverential fear our King was here.

The true presence of the King of Glory; The true surrender of His children is overwhelming.

Expect a True move of God from the inside out.. Come be Awakened and filled. Holy is the Lamb that has been slain.

I have now truly been in the Holy of Holies I have been consumed by the Holy Fire,

To describe the Holies of Holies was like a flame of white and blue, Then as I got closer yellow/orange

And the consumption of the Holiness of Purity of Fire, Pure Peace as I was being consumed. Strength, clean, whole, Newness, Purpose. Love and Peace

MY MEDITATIONS

Numbers 6

'*Y'varekh'kha ADONAI v'yishmerekha.*
[May ADONAI bless me and keep me.]
²⁵ *Ya'er ADONAI panav eleikha vichunekka.*
[May ADONAI make his face shine on
me and show me his favor.]
²⁶ *Yissa ADONAI panav eleikha v'yasem l'kha shalom.*
[May ADONAI lift up his face toward me and give me Peace.]'

<u>Complete Jewish Bible</u> (CJB)

I said,

But there is an **Elah (Awesome Fearful One)** in heaven who reveals secrets (To me). "Praise **Eloah's (Mighty Powerful One)** name from everlasting to everlasting because You are wise and powerful. You changes times and periods of history. You removes kings and establishes them. For the kingdom of God consists of *and* is based on not talk but power (moral power and excellence of soul). And You said, unto me it is given to know the mysteries of the kingdom of God: but to others in parables; that seeing they might not see, and hearing they might not understand. So shall my word be that goes forth out of my mouth: it shall not return to me void [without producing any effect, useless], but it shall accomplish that which I please *and* purpose, and it shall prosper in the thing for which I sent it. You gives wisdom to me because I am wise, I have knowledge and insight. You reveals deeply hidden

---

things. I knows what is in the dark, and light lives in me. God has revealed those things to me by His Spirit. The Spirit searches everything, especially the deep things of God. You alone created my inner being. You knitted me together inside my mother. I will give thanks to You because I have been so amazingly and miraculously made (Today my body is like when I was born with all parts). Your works are miraculous, and my soul is fully aware of this. O **Yahweh,** you are my **Elohim (Judge and Creator)**. I will highly honor you; I will praise your name. You have done miraculous things. You have been completely reliable in carrying out your plans from long ago. Therefore Yahweh tells me, stop being worried *or* being anxious (perpetually uneasy, distracted) about my life, as to what I will eat or what I will drink; nor about my body, as to what I will wear. Is life not more than food, and the body more than clothing? I look at the birds of the air; they neither sow [seed] nor reap [the harvest] nor gather [the crops] into barns, and yet my heavenly Father keeps feeding them. Am I not worth much more than they? And who of us by worrying can add one hour to [the length of] his life? And why are we worried about clothes? See how the lilies *and* wildflowers of the field grow; they do not labor nor do they spin [wool to make clothing], yet Adonai say to me that not even Solomon in all his glory *and* splendor dressed himself like one of these. But if God so clothes the grass of the field, which is alive *and* green today and tomorrow is [cut and] thrown [as fuel] into the furnace, *will You* not much more *clothe* me? I of Great faith! Therefore I will not worry *or* be anxious (perpetually uneasy, distracted), saying, 'What am I going to eat?' or 'What am I going to drink?' or 'What am I going to wear?' For the [pagan] Gentiles eagerly seek all these things; [but I will not worry,] for my heavenly Father knows that I need them. I first *and* most importantly seek (aim at, strive after) Yahweh kingdom and Yahweh righteousness [Your way of doing and being right—the attitude and character of God], and all these things will be given to me also. "Yahweh has put His Spirit within me and cause me to walk in His statutes, and I will be careful to observe *Yahweh* ordinances. I always keep **Yahweh** in front of me. When he is by my side, I cannot be moved. Yes, I keep this book of the *(Scriptures)* on my lips, and meditate on it day and night, so that I will take care to act according to everything that is written in it. Then my undertakings will prosper, and I will succeed. Yahweh have ordered me, 'Be strong, be bold, so I will not be afraid or downhearted, because ADONAI my God is with me wherever I go. "I am strong and courageous! I am not afraid or discouraged [because of what I see with my eyes] for there is a power far greater on my side! In all these things I am a super conquerors, through the one who has loved me. For I am convinced that neither death nor life, neither angels nor other heavenly rulers, neither what exists nor what is coming, neither powers above nor powers below, nor any other created thing will be able to separate me from the love of God which comes to me through the Messiah Yeshua, my Lord. But I have received power when the Holy Spirit came to me. I will be Yeshua witnesses to testify about Him in Jerusalem, throughout Judea and Samaria, and to the ends of the earth." I can do all things through Yeshua who gives me power. This is why the Father loves me: because I lay down my life — in order to take it up again! No one takes it away from me; on the contrary, I lay it down of my own free will. I have the power to lay it down, and I have the power to take it up again. This is what my Father commanded me to do. Yahweh have giving light to the eyes of my hearts, so that I will understand the hope to which You has called me, You has fill me with Your rich glories which is in the inheritance that Yahweh has promised me (Today I receive my inheritance). The Lord is gracious and FULL of compassion (toward me), slow to anger and abounding in mercy and loving-kindness (toward me). I am Your sheep that listen to Your voice, I recognize You, I follow You. And You give me eternal life. I will absolutely never be destroyed, and no one will snatch me from Yeshua hands. I will not be upset by evildoers or envious of those who do wrong, for soon they will wither like grass and fade like the green in the fields. I trust in ADONAI, and do good, I settle in the land, and feed on faithfulness. Then I will delight myself in ADONAI, and he will give to me, my heart's desire. I commit my way to ADONAI and trust in Him, and You will act. No one will be able to withstand me as long as I live. Just as Elohim was with Moshe, so Elohim will be with me. Elohim will neither fail me nor abandon me. He will make my vindication shine forth like light, the justice of my cause like the noonday sun. I will be still before ADONAI; wait patiently till he comes. I won't be upset by those whose way succeeds because of their wicked plans. I stop being angry and put aside rage, and won't be upset —because it leads to evil. My light shines in the darkness, and the darkness has not suppressed it. For evildoers will be cut off, but I'm hoping in ADONAI I will inherit the land. Soon the wicked will be no more; I will look for his place, and he won't be there. But I the meek, I will inherit the land and delight myself in abundant peace. Moreover, my God will fill every need of my, according to his glorious wealth, in union with the Messiah Yeshua. Now to Him who is able to [carry out His purpose and] do superabundantly more than all that I dare ask or think [infinitely beyond my greatest prayers, hopes, or dreams], according to Your power that is at work within me. Bless *Adonai*, my soul! Everything in me, bless His Holy Name! Bless *Adonai*, my soul, and forget none of His benefits! You forgives all my offenses, You heals all my diseases, You redeems my life from the pit, You surrounds me with grace and compassion, You contents me with good as long as I live, so that my youth is renewed like an eagle's. *Adonai Elohim* has given me the ability to speak as a man well taught, so that I, with my words, know how to sustain the weary. Each morning You awakens my ear to hear like those who are taught. *Adonai Elohim* has opened my ear, and I neither rebelled nor turned away. May the God of *shalom (Peace)* make me completely holy — may my entire spirit, soul and body be kept blameless for the coming of my Lord Yeshua the Messiah. I grew up. **Yahweh** is with me and didn't let any of my words go **"unfulfilled"**. Let me who love **Yahweh** hate evil. I guards the lives of his godly ones will rescue them from the power of wicked people. Yeshua assure me *and* most solemnly say to me, I says to this mountain, 'Be lifted up and thrown into the sea!' and I do not doubt in my heart [in God's unlimited power], but believes that what I says is going to take place, it will be done for me [in accordance with God's will]. For this reason Yeshua telling me, whatever things I ask for in prayer [in accordance with God's will], believe [with confident trust] that I have received them, and they will be *given* to me. But as for me, I will sing of Your mighty strength *and* power; Yes, I will sing joyfully of Your lovingkindness in the morning; For You have been my stronghold And a refuge in the day of my distress. Evil people do not understand justice, but I who seek **Yahweh** understand everything. I no longer live, but Christ lives in me. The life I now live I live by believing in God's Son, who loved me and took the punishment for my sins. But I, walk *habitually* in the [Holy] Spirit [seek Him and be responsive to His guidance], and then I will certainly not carry out the desire of the sinful nature [which responds impulsively without regard for God and His precepts]. But I am guided *and* led by the Spirit, I am not subject to the Law. But my spiritual nature produces love, joy, peace, patience, kindness, goodness, faithfulness, gentleness, and self-control. There are no laws against things like these. I who belong to Christ **Yeshua** have crucified my corrupt nature along with its passions and desires. I live by the spiritual nature, then my life is to be conform to the spiritual nature. Your word is a lamp for my foot and light on my path. Then Yeshua said to me, "As I go throughout the world, proclaim the Good News to all creation. Whoever trusts and is immersed will be saved; whoever does not trust will be condemned. And these signs will accompany me because I trust: in Your Name I will drive out demons, speak with new tongues, not be injured if I handle snakes or drink poison, and I will heal the sick by laying hands on them." When I am speaking these Words *Ruach HaKodesh,* fall on *all* who is hearing the message. Now, I didn't receive the spirit that belongs to the world. Instead, I received the Spirit who comes from YAH so that I could know the things which God has freely given me. I don't speak about these things using teachings that are based on intellectual arguments like people do. Instead, I use the Spirit's teachings. I explain spiritual things to those who have the Spirit. Then **Yahweh** stretched out his hand and touched my mouth. **Yahweh** said to me, "Now Yahweh have put His words in my mouth. Today He have put me in charge of nations and kingdoms. I will uproot and tear down. I will destroy and overthrow. I will build and plant." When I had spoken these things, I lifted up my eyes to heaven and said, Father, the hour has come. Glorify *and* exalt *and* honor *and* magnify Your Son, so that Your Son may glorify *and* extol *and* honor *and* magnify You. For it is written, I am holy, for *Yeshua* is holy. **Yeshua** called me and gave me power and authority over every demon and power and authority to cure diseases. He sent me to spread the message about the kingdom of God and to cure the sick. May grace and *shalom* be my in full measure, as I come to a full knowledge of God and Yeshua my Lord. God's power has given me everything I need for life and godliness, through my knowing the One who called me to his own glory and goodness. By these he has given me valuable and superlatively great promises, so that through them I come to share in Yahweh nature and escape the corruption which evil desires have brought into the world. Yahweh said My son, do not forget His teachings, and keep His commands in mind, because they will bring me long life, good years, and peace.

I do not let mercy and truth leave me. I Fasten them around my neck. I write them on the tablet of my heart. Then I will find favor and much success in the sight of **Elohim** and humanity. I trust **Yahweh** with all my heart, and I do not rely on my own understanding. In all my ways I acknowledge him, and he will make my paths smooth. I do not consider myself wise. I fear **Yahweh**, and turn away from evil. Then my body is healed, and my bones have nourishment. I honor **Yahweh** with my wealth and with the first and best part of all my income. My barns are full, and my vats overflow with fresh wine. Behold, Yahweh will bring me health and cure, and Yahweh will cure me, and will reveal unto me the abundance of peace and truth. And it shall be to Yahweh a name of joy, a praise and an honor before all the nations of the earth, which shall hear all the good that You did unto me: and they shall fear and tremble for all the goodness and for all the prosperity that Yahweh procure unto me. I do not reject the discipline of **Yahweh**, He said my son, and do not resent My warning, because **Yahweh** warns me the one he love, even as a father warns a son with whom he is pleased. Blessed is I, the one who finds wisdom and the one who obtains understanding. The Spirit of the Sovereign LORD is on me, because the LORD has anointed me to proclaim good news to the poor. He has sent me to bind up the brokenhearted, to proclaim freedom for the captives and release from darkness for the prisoners, I drive out demons by the Spirit of God, now the Kingdom of God has come upon me! "Neither do they say, 'Behold, here it is!' and 'Behold, from here to there!', for behold, the Kingdom of God is within me. But He, the Spirit of Truth, has comes, *Ruach HaKodesh* will guide me into all the truth [full and complete truth]. For He will not speak on His own initiative, but He will speak whatever He hears [from the Father—the message regarding the Son], and *Ruach HaKodesh* will disclose to me, what is to come [in the future]. He will glorify *and* honor the Son, because He (the Holy Spirit) will take from what is Yeshua and will disclose it to me. All things that the Father has are mine. Because of this I said that He [the Spirit] will take from what is Yeshuah and will reveal it to me. But Yahweh will heal me and restore me to health. Yahweh will heal, and Yahweh will give me peace and security. I call unto Yahweh, and He will answer me, and shew me great and mighty things, which I knowest not. Heaven belongs to *Adonai*, but the earth he has given to me (humankind). And as I go, preach, saying, The kingdom of heaven is at hand. I will heal the sick, cleanse the lepers, raise the dead, cast out devils: freely I have received, freely I give. I that dwelleth in the secret place of the most High shall abide under the shadow of the Almighty. I will say of the LORD, He is my refuge and my fortress: my God; in him will I trust. Surely he shall deliver me from the snare of the fowler, and from the noisome pestilence. He shall cover me with his feathers, and under his wings I shalt trust: his truth shall be my shield and buckler. I shalt not be afraid for the terror by night; nor for the arrow that flieth by day; Nor for the pestilence that walketh in darkness; nor for the destruction that wasteth at noonday. A thousand shall fall at my side, and ten thousand at my right hand; but it shall not come nigh thee. Only with my eyes shalt thou behold and see the reward of the wicked. Because I have made the LORD, which is my refuge, even the most High, my habitation; there shall no evil befall me, neither shall any plague come near my dwelling. For Yahweh shall give his angels charge over me, to keep me in all my ways. They shall bear me up in their hands, lest I dash my foot against a stone. I shall tread upon the lion and adder: the young lion and the dragon shall I trample under feet. Because he hath set his love upon me, therefore will He deliver me: Yahweh will set me on high, because I hath known His Name. I shall call upon Elohim, and He will answer me: Yahweh will be with me in trouble; He will deliver me, and honor me. With long life will Yahweh satisfy me, and shew me His salvation. **Scriptures are from Complete Jewish Bible (CJB)**Was inspired by the Holy Spirit

THE WINDS OF CHANGE

part 2

4/24/2016
0800

The Winds of change have come....
Can you feel it?
The power of My Holy Spirit has Come
Now with this wind of change comes..
The Rising of MY Sons
Sons of God Rise up in MY Power
My Righteousness and most of all My Love
The Wind of Change has come to motivate
MY body into oneness of Spirit ... Unity and Love

The Wind of Change

part 3

7/11/2016
1:32 am

The Wind of Change have come My Son
The winds have come, on this wind of change...
The Time of Change is here; The Time of Blessing and the
end of curses. The time of Growth move with this Wind
of Change, your molting is almost complete. Says the
Lord. You My son, mount up as an Eagle let your wings
spread test the Wind. I AM the Wind Beneath your wings
ABBA

9/14/2016
5:15am

Burning Love
The winds of Fire swirl around me.
It burns out my shame and fear
The winds of Fire blow on the embers of my heart;
Reigniting The Burning Love for My Father.
No more fear or shame for the Fire is Holy
Burning Love, Burning Love, Pure and Clean, Holy
The Winds of Fire are changing me,
engulfing me over taking me
I raise my hands in worship and adoration; Tears
swell in my eyes for His Love overwhelms me.
Never have I felt this not by a human, this Love
Pierces right to the core of my heart, Burning up
the lies of my past, cleansing me, blowing the chaff
away. Wind of Fire swirl around and in me….
Don't ever let me go… Burning Love

12/2/2016

It is Time
My soul Aches
My heart shattered in Pieces
My mind a mess
Realizing the mess, I have made for my disobedience
to the God of Heaven and earth YHWH.
Working on making it right by God hurts
me and the Truth hurts others
I will No longer live in deception or lies
When God says Time is up … Time is up
Sin has its season and I may ache but am
thankful I was shown the Truth..
This way I can be free from my sin and walk as a
man of Valor to my King, Savior and Friend.
I need to listen to God alone and Stop being swayed by
the Religious men and women saying this or that.
IT IS TIME to be obedient to God and stop listening to man.
GOD IS SOVERN

2/4/2019

Being Real
The Darkness is Real
The Loneliness is Real
The Feeling of a heart shattered in Pieces is Real
The tears are Real
The thoughts of dying are Real
The question why am I here is so Real
What is my purpose
Why do people lie and say they care
when there action is otherwise?
They only speak words with no action
What is there to live for?
When you don't care anymore..
The one you love rarely speaks to you
Why go on?
Hope has been destroyed

New Poem .....
I long for Love.....
A Love that last forever A love that last for eternity
A Love were we just gaze into each other's eyes and
be able to see the Light of God in each other.
I so Long for Love
To have someone to be in Love with me.
My heart cries night after night unto God
Tears roll down my face like a waterfall until
my head throbs so hard it hurts.
Why GOD why I cry out
So much pain so much torment
Where is this Love I read about from the depths of Heaven
I need to be Loved ...
I need to feel the true embrace of Love...
I so Long for LOVE.....

5:35
2/17/2017

Declaration over Israel
We Declare Yeshua the Messiah over the
Tribes of Israel and all of Jerusalem
We Declare Peace over Jerusalem
We Declare the Love of YAH over Israel and Jerusalem
We Declare Adonai is over Jerusalem
We Declare our Love for Israel and Jerusalem
We Declare we are in grafted into the vine of YAH
We Declare the Victory of the Messiah over Jerusalem
this Day In the Name of My KING YASHUA/ Jesus
AMEN

Breaking Generational Curses

In the Name of Yeshua I repent for all generational idolatry
I repent for all personal and generational rebellion, stubbornness and disobedience that have contributed to witchcraft in my life and my generational blood line.
I repent for all and any worship of myself or any need of personal recognition
I repent for all any envy and jealousy of spiritual giftings of others and any in my generational blood line to 5 generations back
I repent for myself and for those in my generational bloodline that did not guard the Spiritual heritage of the gate of our spiritual and physical senses.
I repent for choosing my will above the will of YWHW

Today I choose to cast off the works of darkness off myself and 5 generations back and put on the Armor of Light the Messiah Yeshua

I choose to walk according to the grace and anointing the Messiah has placed on my life

I choose to take back all Generational blessings Spiritually, Physically and financially 5 generations back that have been discarded.

Yeshua will you now remove all ungodly spiritual beings and people not benefitting the Anointing and Grace you bestowed on me

Remove any generational curses of witchcraft rebellion or idolatry or jealousy in Yeshua's name

I declare Yeshua is head and God over all

Prayer based on Ez. 8:1-6, Romans 12;3 Eph. 4 John 17 Romans 13 Psalm 18

The last activity Jesus Christ shared with His disciples, only hours before He was crucified, was the biblically commanded Passover celebration. He had observed this festival annually since His birth (Luke 2:41).

Accompanied by His 12 apostles for their final Passover meal together, "He said to them, '*With fervent desire* I have desired to eat this Passover with you before I suffer'" (Luke 22:15, emphasis added throughout). His intense longing to observe this Passover service reveals His deep devotion to celebrating it.

Not only does Jesus—merely hours before His crucifixion—still regard keeping the Passover as important, but also, as He explained to His disciples that evening, He fully intends to observe it with them again when "it is fulfilled in the kingdom of God" (Luke 22:16).

Why did Jesus set such a committed example of observing this festival if He intended soon afterward—as is commonly believed today—to abolish this festival? Does that really make any sense?

Most people claiming to follow Christ's example today know little or nothing about the Passover or the other biblically commanded festivals. Nor do they understand why He considered them important. And most of them certainly have never thought of these days as meaningful to them personally. But should they?

ACKNOWLEDGEMENTS

First off I want to give God all Honor and Glory
Because He is the one and only True God there is No other.
Jesus Christ for saving my soul from damnation.
The Holy Spirit for the wisdom and
guidance to do this book.

Amen.

CPSIA information can be obtained
at www.ICGtesting.com
Printed in the USA
BVHW071114060519
547457BV00004B/841/P